YOU SHOULD MEET

Misty Copeland

T0033864

by Laurie Calkhoven
illustrated by Monique Dong

Ready-to-Read

Simon Spotlight
New York   London   Toronto   Sydney   New Delhi

SIMON SPOTLIGHT
An imprint of Simon & Schuster Children's Publishing Division
1230 Avenue of the Americas, New York, New York 10020
This Simon Spotlight edition December 2020
Text copyright © 2016 by Simon & Schuster, Inc.
Illustrations copyright © 2016 by Monique Dong
All rights reserved, including the right of reproduction in whole or in part in any form.
SIMON SPOTLIGHT, READY-TO-READ, and colophon are registered trademarks
of Simon & Schuster, Inc.
For information about special discounts for bulk purchases, please contact Simon & Schuster Special Sales at
1-866-506-1949 or business@simonandschuster.com.
Manufactured in China 0920 LEO

CONTENTS

Introduction

Have you ever dreamed of being a ballerina? Have you wondered about the hard work that goes into twirling across a stage, or flying through the air in a giant leap? What if you looked different from all the ballerinas you'd ever seen, but you knew in your heart you should be one?

If you've ever wondered about those things, then you should meet Misty Copeland. Misty is the first African American woman to earn the position of principal dancer, the highest level a dancer can achieve, in the American Ballet Theatre. She has also inspired young people all over the world to go after their **dreams**.

Welcome to California

Chapter 1
Before Ballet

Misty was born on September 10, 1982, in Kansas City, Missouri. She had three older siblings, two brothers and a sister. When Misty was two, her mother left her father. The family took a bus across the United States to San Pedro, California. Misty wouldn't see her father again until she was grown up.

From then on, Misty was on the move. Her mother married and divorced two more times and had two more children. Each time her mother divorced, the family moved to a new house.

Misty enjoyed being part of a big family, but all the changes made her feel worried. She worried most about making mistakes at school. She made up for that by getting to school an hour early every morning. She studied and got good grades.

Life wasn't all school, though. Misty loved to watch gymnastics on television. She taught herself to do cartwheels, backbends, and other moves.

Dancing around the house to Mariah Carey's music videos also made Misty happy. When she was in middle school, she *choreographed* a dance (that means she created a sequence of steps and moves) for herself and her two best friends. They danced in the school talent show.

Misty loved being onstage. "I felt fierce," she later wrote in her autobiography.

Chapter 2
First Steps

Middle school brought Misty new challenges. She decided to try to win a place on the school's *drill team* like her sister, Erica, had done before her. A drill team performs dance moves for a school audience. Misty wanted to be more than just part of the team. She wanted to be the captain.

Misty created her own routine and danced her best. One night she got a phone call from the team's coach, Elizabeth Cantine. Misty was named captain of the drill team! She loved being team captain. Practice was one place where she didn't feel worried.

Coach Cantine had a background in ballet. She taught Misty some ballet moves for the drill team and saw how good Misty was. She gave Misty the idea of taking a ballet class at the local Boys & Girls Club.

The Boys & Girls Club was another place where Misty didn't feel worried. The Boys & Girls Club is a safe place where kids can go after school to play sports, be creative, and have fun. Misty and her brothers and sisters went to the local club almost every day after school.

Misty wanted to make her coach happy. Even though she knew nothing about ballet, she went to the class. She didn't have a leotard or tights or ballet shoes. For two weeks Misty sat and watched the ballet dancers. She was afraid she would look silly if she tried to dance. But one day she did try, wearing her gym clothes and dancing in her socks.

Most serious ballerinas start dancing by the time they are seven years old. Misty was thirteen when she started. Her ballet teacher, Cindy Bradley, saw Misty's talent from the very beginning. She knew right away that Misty was a special dancer. It wasn't long before Misty left the Boys & Girls Club to dance every day in Cindy's ballet studio.

Chapter 3
Becoming a Ballerina

Soon Misty started to feel like a ballerina. She took classes with dancers who had been training for years, and kept up with them. Within a few months she was dancing *en pointe,* or on the tips of her toes. It takes most dancers years to develop this skill. In just a few months Misty was dancing difficult steps and soaring past the other dancers.

At the same time, things were not good at home. Misty's second stepfather often said hurtful things to her mother and to her siblings. The family left him and moved into a small motel room next to a busy highway.

Misty got a ride to the ballet studio with Cindy after school every day, but she had to take a long bus ride home. By then ballet was more than a hobby for Misty. The world of ballet was a place where she felt safe and happy, a place where she was able to shine. The ballet classes were worth the hour-long bus ride home every night.

Misty's mother saw how hard her daughter worked. She saw how tired Misty was. She told Misty it was too much, she'd have to give up ballet. Misty was heartbroken. The next day she cried as she told Cindy she couldn't come back to class.

Cindy told Misty's mother that Misty had a chance to be a star. Cindy didn't want Misty to leave class. Together Cindy and Misty's mother decided that Misty would live with Cindy during the week to be closer to school and at the motel with her family on weekends.

Misty's weekends were often busy with performances. She spent less and less time with her family. After almost three years Misty's mother told Misty that it was time to come home.

Both Misty's mother and Cindy thought they knew what was best for Misty. Misty's mother wanted her to move back home. Cindy wanted Misty to continue to live with her and to dance. The two women went to court and asked the court to decide where Misty should live. Misty was scared and sad. She wanted to make everyone happy.

Chapter 4
Misty Takes New York by Storm

The court decided that Misty would move back in with her family and take lessons at a new studio closer to home after school. After a few months her mother got a better job and they moved out of the motel. Misty soon settled into her new ballet studio, even though she missed her old friends and teachers.

Misty continued to learn in her new studio. The following year she was invited to a summer program at the American Ballet Theatre (ABT) in New York City. ABT is one of the best ballet companies in the world.

Misty had wanted to dance for ABT ever since she had seen Paloma Herrera dance with the ballet company in the 1990s. Paloma was one of the youngest stars in the history of ABT. She was fifteen when she moved from Argentina to New York to join the *corps de ballet*, the group of dancers in the background of ballet performances. Two years later she was promoted to soloist. When she was nineteen, Paloma became a principal dancer.

Misty knew that she had started dancing too late to become a principal dancer at nineteen, but she wanted to follow Paloma's path. If she made it to Paloma's level, she would be the first

African American woman to do so in the history of the American Ballet Theatre.

Now Misty was going to dance for the same ballet company in New York City. "I was ready to take the Big Apple by storm," Misty wrote in her autobiography. And she did. After she completed the summer program, ABT invited her to join them full-time.

It was a hard decision, but Misty decided to go home and finish her last year of high school. She hoped that ABT would make her the same offer the

following summer. And they did.

Misty became a member of the corps de ballet. She was the only African American woman out of eighty dancers. She worried that she would never fit in.

The days were long and hard. Misty took a ninety-minute ballet class every morning and then rehearsed for seven hours.

At night the dancers performed.

By the end of her first year, Misty was beginning to work her way up in the company. Then one day while she was dancing, pain exploded in her back. The stress of dancing had injured a bone in Misty's spine. For the next year she wore a back brace for twenty-three hours a day and couldn't dance.

During that year Misty's body changed. She became curvier than she had been before. Once she was able to dance again, she had to learn how to dance all over again in her new body. People began to tell her that she was too "athletic" to be a

ballerina. Her strong muscles stood out.

No one said that there wasn't a place in ballet for an African American woman, but Misty knew some people thought that. She just kept dancing and showed them how **graceful and strong** she was.

Six years after she joined the corps de ballet, Misty was named a *soloist*. A soloist is a performer with a special role in the ballet. It had been over twenty years since an African American woman had had that honor at American Ballet Theatre. The first African American women soloists had been Nora Kimball and Shelley Washington, who had joined the company as soloists in the 1980s. Now Misty's name was being added to that short list.

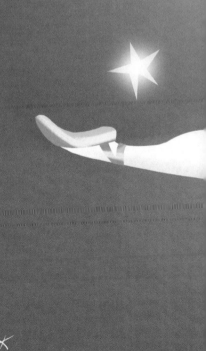

Chapter 5
Twirling into History

It wasn't long before Misty was standing out because of her incredible dancing. People outside the ballet world noticed her too.

Misty starred in a commercial for a sportswear company. In the commercial a little girl read a letter listing all the reasons why she could never be a ballerina, such as having the wrong body type for ballet, and at age thirteen she was too old to be considered. As the girl spoke, Misty twirled and leapt across the stage. Within one week, more than four million people had watched the commercial on the Internet.

The support of Misty's friends and fans helped her to keep doing the hard work to win the best roles in the ballet company. In the spring of 2012 Misty was picked for the lead role in *The Firebird*, a famous ballet. Misty was the first African American woman ever to dance the role for a major ballet company, and she earned rave reviews. But dancing had also caused another injury. Misty needed surgery to repair fractures in her leg.

Some doctors said she would never dance again. But Misty didn't give up. She worked hard and got better, and danced more roles, including the lead role in *Swan Lake*. The lead in *Swan Lake* is the role every ballerina imagines herself performing. Dancing this role was a dream come true.

Misty also wrote her autobiography, and a separate picture book called *Firebird*.

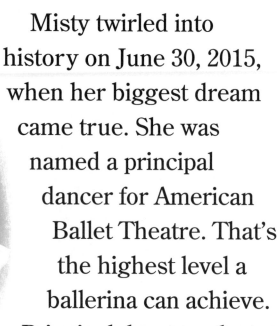

Misty twirled into history on June 30, 2015, when her biggest dream came true. She was named a principal dancer for American Ballet Theatre. That's the highest level a ballerina can achieve. Principal dancers almost always get the biggest roles in ballet. Their pictures are also published in the ballet programs, and young dancers all over the world look up to them. Misty is the first African American woman to be a principal dancer in ABT's history.

What's next for this unstoppable ballerina? Only time will tell, but it's clear that Misty will continue to inspire young people to go after their dreams. A few days after being named principal dancer, she said, "You can dream big, and it doesn't matter what you look like, where you come from, what your background is. That's the example that I want to set and what I want to leave behind."

Now that you've met Misty Copeland, wouldn't you agree that anything is possible?

Dream big!

BUT WAIT . . .

THERE'S MORE!

Turn the page to learn more about ballet.

Learn the finer *pointes* of the five basic positions!

Lesson number one for any ballet dancer is how to hold their arms and legs. Sounds easy, right? There are five basic positions, and all of them take years of practice to get just right. If you try these positions at home, be careful and don't attempt to force your toes to turn all the way out to the side! It takes dancers many years of training to get their hips turned out enough that their toes point to the side. You can injure yourself if you try to force your legs into an unnatural position.

In first position the dancer's heels are together and their toes are pointed outward. This outward positioning of the feet is called *turn-out*. When a dancer first begins learning ballet, their feet will form a V in first position. As they slowly progress, the opening of the V will widen until their feet form a straight line. It takes many years of training to safely achieve a 180-degree turn-out. In first position the arms are held in front of the dancer, either an inch or two from the thighs or out in front of the stomach. The fingers should almost touch, and the arms should be rounded, as if the dancer were holding a beach ball.

In second position the dancer's

heels are a few inches apart, and their toes are pointed outward. The arms are still slightly rounded but are held out to the sides.

In **third position** one foot is in front of the other. The heel of the front foot touches the arch, or middle of the back foot. The toes are pointed outward. One arm is raised above the head. The other arm is held out to the side. Third position for the feet is rarely used because it's so similar to fifth position, but third position for the arms is used regularly.

In **fourth position** one foot is a few inches in front of the other, and the toes are pointed outward. If the right foot is in front, the right arm is raised above the head and the left is held out in front.

In **fifth position** the feet are arranged the same as they are in third position, except the front foot covers the whole back foot. Both arms are slightly rounded and held above the head, with the fingers almost touching.

The History of Ballet

Ballet began as a party activity in fifteenth-century Italy, during the *Renaissance* (say: REN-nah-sance), a time when people in Europe were very interested in art and literature. The nobility and court wore fancy masks and danced for their guests. The steps were arranged by a dancing master.

Settings, costumes, and even poetry were added to ballet performances in sixteenth-century France with *ballet de cour* (court ballet). The dancers wore masks and long ball gowns, and the way they moved was very different from how modern-day ballerinas move.

King Louis XIV was the first to hire professional ballet dancers. He was a fan of the pastime and played many roles himself. When he couldn't dance anymore, he paid the best performers to entertain him. Suddenly, ballet became a career.

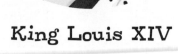

King Louis XIV

In the mid-1700s Jean-Georges Noverre had the idea to tell a story through movement, the way an opera told a story through song. He created *ballet d'action*, and the art form took to the stage.

In the mid-nineteenth century, ballets such as *Giselle* called for gently floating spirits and fairies. To create this illusion, ballerinas wore flowing skirts and skimmed the floor in newly invented pointe shoes.

The second half of the nineteenth century brought us *The Nutcracker*, *The Sleeping Beauty*, and *Swan Lake*. Ballerinas' flowing skirts became short tutus, and dancers showed off complex pointe work, high leg lifts, and the elegant movements we see today.

Ballet has continued to grow and change. George Balanchine's (say: bal-an-SHEEN) ballets expressed ideas without telling stories. Martha Graham pioneered modern dance. Alvin Ailey helped popularize modern dance and brought African American culture into the spotlight on ballet's biggest stages.

In addition to those we've mentioned, we can thank countless individuals for transforming ballet from a Renaissance pastime into a celebrated and

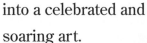

soaring art.

Ballet by the Numbers

• Ballet dancers who aspire to dance professionally take up to 15 classes per week and usually begin training when they are 7 years old.

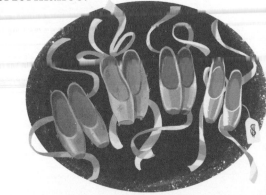

• A professional dancer (someone who earns a living by dancing) usually retires when he or she is 30 to 40 years old.

• An average professional ballerina can go through 6 pairs of pointe shoes a week and 1 pair per performance.

• A pair of pointe shoes costs about $50 to $80.

- The average ballerina trains for 8 to 10 years before becoming a professional.

- The average professional ballet dancer is practicing, rehearsing, and performing for 7 to 10 hours each day.

- American Ballet Theatre employed 18 principals, 13 soloists, and 57 corps de ballet dancers as of September 2015.

- In addition to the 5 basic positions, ballet dancers must learn the 8 positions of the body used in performances.

- One of the most famous ballet choreographers, George Balanchine, created 465 works in his lifetime.

Now that you've met Misty, what have you learned?

1. In what year was Misty born?

a. 1932　　　　　　　　b. 1952　　　　　　　　c. 1982

2. Misty's life has been "on the move" since she was two years old. What does that mean?

a. She has experienced many changes since then.

b. She started taking ballet lessons when she was two years old.

c. Since she learned to walk, she's had a hard time sitting still.

3. For how long did Misty train before she was dancing en pointe, or on the tips of her toes?

a. A few days　　　　　　b. A few months　　　　　c. A year

4. When did Misty realize she wanted to dance for American Ballet Theatre?

a. When she moved to New York　b. When she saw Paloma Herrera perform

c. During her first ballet class

5. What did Misty mean when she said she was ready to "take the Big Apple by storm?"

a. She wanted to become a star in New York City.

b. She wanted to tour San Francisco as quickly as possible.

c. She wanted to fly over Manhattan.

6. When people said Misty was too "athletic" to be a ballerina, what did they mean?

a. She spent too much time at the gym instead of rehearsal.

b. She stood out because she was an awkward dancer.

c. She didn't look like a ballerina because her muscles stood out.

7. What was historical about Misty's being promoted to principal dancer at American Ballet Theatre?

a. She was the first African American dancer admitted to the company.

b. She was the first African American woman to be made principal dancer at the company.

c. She had the greatest number of injuries of any American Ballet Theatre principal dancer.

8. Misty says she wants to set an example. What is that example?

a. Practice makes perfect.　　　　b. A ballerina can achieve anything.

c. You can dream big no matter what your background is.

Answers: 1. c　2. a　3. b　4. b　5. a　6. c　7. b　8. c